Songs In

Diminishment

ESSAYS AND POEMS

Mildred Sherk Kreider

There is a singer everyone has heard,
Loud, a mid-summer bird,
Who makes the solid tree trunks sound again.
He says that leaves are old and that for flowers
Mid-summer is to spring as one to ten.
He says the early petal-fall is past
When pear and cherry bloom went down in showers
On sunny days a moment overcast.
And comes that other fall we name the fall.
He says the highway dust is over all.
The bird would cease and be as other birds
But that he knows in singing not to sing,
The question that he frames in all but words
Is what to make of a diminished thing.

-"The Oven Bird"
Robert Frost

CONTENTS

SONGS IN
DIMINISHMENT

FIRST SONG OF DIMINISHMENT

It's going to get worse. Look at what is here, not what is gone.

The first difficult birthday for me was the twenty-third. Because, you see, I didn't live happily ever after. In my family of origin, birthdays were always celebrated with the best homemade chocolate cake you ever tasted, and a birthday card with a one-dollar bill inside. As long as she lived, Mom made sure that her children's birthdays didn't pass without these two ingredients.

So at first I loved birthday celebrations. The future was rosy. Growing up I liked stories with a happy ending. Even when I was in college I liked stories where they all lived happily ever after. I met Prince Charming and fell in love. For a while I felt that I would live happily ever after.

Then there was the year of my twenty-third birthday. I had graduated from college. Prince C. and I had married. And then I went to work on a surgical ward, evening shift, in Elkhart General Hospital and I had another birthday. And it looked like birthdays were just going to continue. I hadn't read the whole script. The only thing I was sure of was that Prince C and I would get older.

But the world was full of possibilities. Sid and I enjoyed life together. I remember how much energy Sid and I put into a Christmas celebration when our daughter was six. We moved into an old stone house on a 70-acre farm. We had gifts and parties and meals with extended family members and friends, snow and sledding and all of the wonderful gifts we could bring to life from storybooks. Everything was really great. We promised our children that it would be. When it was all over I sat down on the floor in front the ashes of a dying fire in the living room fireplace and Mary Elizabeth snuggled up beside me. She asked: "Is this all there is?"

I think it was around my 30th birthday that I began to think seriously about my mortality. My friends were bemoaning their first wrinkles. I don't remember where we were, perhaps it was in church when Sid reached over and lightly traced a line along my cheek with the back of his fingers. He put his hand down without a comment.

And I thought: Why is that first wrinkle so unwelcome? I guessed that it was because the wrinkle was objective evidence of aging, and I told myself a story.

Once upon a time people were born with super-wrinkled skin covering them. As they grew up they lost their wrinkles and, in time, just before they died, they had totally smooth skin. These people got hysterical as their skin smoothed out and spent a lot of time and money trying to make it look wrinkled.

But the wrinkled skin approach did not work for me. So I tried another approach. On my thirtieth birthday I thought, *If I imagine myself at the end of my life, looking back at thirty, I will see it as a very vital, energetic time. I will live the thirties with more awareness of their potential.* That became a more effective way for me to deal with the anxiety of aging.

I read that Robert Frost took eight years to write "The Oven Bird," and finished it when he was 40. In it, he puzzles over what to do "with a diminished thing." People find differing meanings in the poem. I find in it a challenge to look for the lyrical in diminishment. The statements in the poem are matter-of-fact: there is a singer; everyone has heard him. But he doesn't sing. He doesn't have a lyrical voice; he has a declarative voice. He states facts: he says that it is midsummer; he says the seasons are progressing; he says that the dust of the highway is falling on everything. There is something relentless in the flow of seasons in "The Oven Bird."

I ask, is there no song in the fall? Is there no song in diminishment? I read this poem as a search for meaning, and I search for the lyrical in diminishment.

HALLUCINATIONS

I think it was in 2010 that I first hallucinated.

Apparently it is not uncommon for people with Parkinson's Disease ("PD") to have hallucinations, related to either the disease or the treatment. For me, it began several years after I was diagnosed, when I was admitted to our community hospital unconscious, in septic shock. I don't remember being in intensive care, although I spent several days there. It was in the step down unit that I saw graffiti scribbled across the ceiling of my room. There was more graffiti on the hospital television screen. I could see it clearly, and I knew it wasn't there.

Several weeks later, back home on our farm, I awoke one night and looked out of my bedroom window. In the shadows by the barn I saw shapes of people and things. I couldn't tell what they were, so I called Gary.

Gary was a neighbor and a long-time member of the neighborhood church I attended. He was retired, and spent his summers in a small house trailer at the head of the Chesapeake Bay. He was a handyman who could fix anything, and an outdoorsman who hunted deer and Canada geese on my farm. I always had a good supply of fresh venison, wild geese and seafood from the eastern shore. He showed me how to catch crabs. At the farm one day in hunting season, we were sitting on the porch and he had his gun in his hand, when several Canada geese settled on the pond. Gary stood, picked up his gun, and quietly walked toward the pond. I had roast goose for dinner that evening.

Gary had said to call him if I was worried about anything, so I called. He was there in ten minutes. He came to the front door and talked with me, walked out to where I had seen something, then came back in. Nothing there, he said. He encouraged me to call again if I saw anything that concerned me.

I went upstairs after he left, looked out of the window and saw the same scary, bloated cartoon figures that looked like inflatable Christmas lawn decorations.

I called Gary again, and he was there right away. He went out, came back in, and said, "Nothing there." I assured him there was something there. I saw it. We walked to the barn together. He walked around the barn and stopped where I had seen something. "Look at the loose dust on the lane," he said. "There are no footprints or other marks here." He was convincing. He went home again, and I went back into the house. I looked out of the window and saw the same scary creatures. There is nothing there, I told myself.

As the morning light came, I could see the shadows and forms of unfamiliar, scary things become the light on the shed behind the sugar maple tree, shadows in the trees, and the light on the farm equipment behind the milk house by the barn.

I tried to analyze my mistakes in vision. It seemed that I first read what I saw as two-dimensional, and the part of my brain that processes visual images guessed what I was looking at from the information available to it. When I was a kid, I learned to read comic strips upside down: when the newspaper was spread out on the floor, my three older siblings took all the space available to read it right side up. I can't read visual displays upside down any more. I even have difficulty if what I am looking at is rotated 90 degrees. It seemed to me that my brain was functioning much like the autocorrect function on my computer; it was interpreting the visual display in front of me and changing it to what it thought it should be. With more light, I saw things correctly. Sometimes when I was hallucinating I wished I could paint what I saw, so that other people would know what I was seeing.

When I first saw Vincent van Gogh's paintings of wheat fields with crows, I was astonished. The series of wheat fields with crows were among the last paintings of van Gogh's life. Throughout his life van Gogh sketched and painted wheat fields in different light and with different techniques to express the different emotions he felt. One painting, evidently painted in early morning with limited light, has a dark red hue. There is no green. There are rows of clouds that make curious shapes, alone and together. In the center he focuses on a lane that curves to the left, dividing the field into two parts. I looked at it and gasped. In the foreground I saw two large, ill-defined, but definitely scary creatures squaring off. I read the tension in this painting as high. But in paintings of the same scene showing the full light of the morning sun—the gold of the wheat, the blue of the sky, the green grass and brown mud in the lane—the effect is pastoral. I read the picture in two different ways, rather like the drawing in Psychology 101 textbooks: is it a beautiful young woman or an old hag? Did van Gogh paint a wheat field with crows or two animals snarling at each other?

Van Gogh was fascinated with the effect of light on pigment, and driven to understand the use of color in painting. He was also afflicted with a malady of the central nervous system that resulted in seizures and visual and auditory hallucinations. I wonder if the desire to understand or share the experience of hallucinating is what motivated van Gogh's series of wheat fields. He does not discuss this in his letters to his brother. Sometimes I think that van Gogh's life work is like a Rosetta Stone, a key to our understanding visual communication in a new way—an alphabet of imagery.

Like van Gogh, I have also had auditory hallucinations. My son Tim once asked me what I hear. I hear sounds like faint funeral home music, I told him. It sounds like organ chords, and I can recognize a given hymn by the sequence and rhythm of the chords being played. The sound was around me wherever I went, like the tune that you can't get out of your head. At first I considered the possibility that someone might be providing the residents of this retirement community with subliminal music to keep us quiet. Tim said, No, Mom.

I found the music very annoying. I could understand how someone could be driven to self-destructive behavior in response to the endless repetition of simple chords. I was relieved to find that if I turned on a competing sound, such as recorded piano music, I no longer heard the auditory hallucination.

I am seldom disturbed by visual or auditory hallucinations now. For one thing, I've moved from the country to the city, and there is more light outside at night. I feel safer in my new location, and perhaps for that reason I don't see threatening things outside. I now expect to have difficulty reading the visual display before me when the lighting is poor, so I reserve judgment on what my brain tells me I'm seeing; I don't try to read things upside down. And I'd like to believe that there can be some healing after damage to the brain.

The experience continues to fascinate me, however. I believe that internal factors, such as emotions, influence—maybe determine—how I see and remember many things. Maybe everything. I used to think that the person standing beside me sees what I see. I used to think that what I see was real and can be counted on. I wondered how other people can be so wrong in their readings of some situations. But perception and thought are specific to the individual, based on what is going on inside her as well as what is going on outside.

I think a flexibility and a redundancy are built into our perceptual systems that bring stability to our perception and enable us to recover and use the information provided by those systems. The brain not only stores information, but determines what information is relevant at a given moment in time.

So: do you see what I see?

So: what are out-of-body experiences?

So: what are the near-death experiences people hold as real and sacred?

What is the relationship between what is happening and what we think is happening? Who is qualified to make that judgment?

For me, these experiences have been another great gift that deepen my awareness of the place and time in which we all live. Life is so much more than what we think it is—much more than what commercials on television tell us it is. And so much more important. Beneath the façade of daily occurrences we sometimes catch a glimpse of the depth of being in our existence.

Despite our belief that life has a discrete past, present and future, I believe that life is a continuous flow of being, in which the past is carried into the present and anticipates the future. Past, present and future are one. When within ourselves we lose the record of the past and anticipation of the future, our being is impoverished. Then the past does not inform the present, and the future must be foraged from the chaos of the present, like searching for substance in shadows.

STORIES FROM THE YOUNGEST

I

I was two or three years old when I became the
only child in the family left at home with Mom
while the others were in school. Years later, I
was the child who moved with my parents to a
new country when the other children were on
their own, in school or employed. Sometimes I
was the only person at home to talk with Mom.
So we spoke of many different things—*"of shoes
and ships and sealing wax, of cabbages and kings."*

Sometimes she told me old family stories passed from one generation to the next. Mom thought her family name was Senor. She was an adult when she learned that the family name was really *Senior*, a name not unknown, but also not common, in Wales. I think it was Mom's grandfather who, as a Senior, had co-signed a loan for his brother, and, when the loan came due, his brother didn't have funds to cover it. Great-grandpa did, but he didn't want it to happen again, so he paid the loan but changed the spelling of his name, to protect himself from his brother's excesses.

The Davis family, another family from Wales, was wealthy. They had several daughters and one son. The son received most of the inheritance. My great-grandmother, one of the daughters, received a small inheritance, with which she bought some expensive glassware that was passed down through the genera-tions by the women of the family. I had several of those pieces; I gave a footed bowl for serving fruit and individual fruit dishes shaped like leaves to a niece.

My mother also gave me a glass that my grandfather had given to my grandmother on their first date. The red glass has her name and the date carved on it. I don't remember what that style of glassware was called. I passed it on to another niece, who lives in Alberta, Canada.

My favorite family story was about another great-grandfather, who owned an orchard. One day all the apples he had taken to the market to sell came back home with him. Not one was sold. Great-grandpa chopped down all his trees. My brother Harold, the soul of reason, argued that this was a perfectly reasonable thing to do. Perhaps it was, if the orchard was old or diseased. Harold argued that Grandpa planned to sell the land for development and that felling the trees made the land more salable. I always liked the family stories about people doing unexpected and unexplained things. As a sometimes-hyperactive child, I liked hearing about less-than-perfect ancestors; they provided space in the family for people like me.

Mom's mother was Florence Senor, née Riggins. Mom was born and grew up in West Berlin, New Jersey, in a house that her father purchased when he married Florence. David and Florence had three children: Elwood D. Senor was the oldest; Mom, Mila Hilda Senor, was the second child, four years younger than Elwood; Edna, the youngest, died as a young child, I think of an infectious disease.

David, a quiet, gentle man, was a stone dresser at the local Sherwin-Williams paint company. He prepared stones to grind pigments for paint. I think his work was difficult; Mom remembered that every Sunday evening he had painful migraine headaches. He died of lung disease when Mom was in her early twenties.

Mom's mother was a homemaker who was also a gifted seamstress. Grandma Senor increased the family income through her skill on a portable electric Singer sewing machine, an early model. Pictures of my mother show that she was an attractive young woman who wore the latest styles. With dark eyes and dark brown hair, olive skin and the family name "Senor," we assumed there were Spanish genes in our background. (We now think that rather than a direct connection to Spain, there might be a connection through our ancestors on the British Isles.)

Mom went to local schools in Voorhees township. When she graduated from high school she was employ-ed by the *Philadelphia Bulletin* daily newspaper as a telephone operator.

Sometimes Mom talked about her family. Mom was the second child in the family, and the first daughter. The family had traditional gender roles; Mom told me that when she was a girl, after dinner in the evening her parents would relax in the living room, as would her brother, Elwood, while she was expected to stay in the kitchen to wash and dry the dishes. She said she cried as she did the dishes and vowed that if she had daughters, she would treat them differently.

Mom never left us in the kitchen by ourselves. Sometimes she was tired by the end of the day, and as we were getting ready to wash dishes she'd say she was tired and wonder whether we would clean up without her, but I'm afraid we never volunteered, and she never assigned us.

"Your father didn't approve of that," she said to me, meaning treating daughters in a non-traditional way. "He said, 'They won't thank you when they grow up.'" In fact I was shocked, as I grew older, to discover that there were certain basic female skills I did not have—and didn't want, for that matter. My mother didn't teach us to cook; she always said it was easier to do it herself. I think her mother liked to cook, and Mom had some favorite recipes from her child-hood that she included in her personal cookbook, like steamed carrot pudding for Christmas din-ner. But she saw that her daughters as well as her sons took moral responsibility for the wel-fare of others, and taught this in our home.

Mom talked about plans and expectations. The local Methodist Episcopal church was the social center of her family and home community, and she was a devout supporter of the church. After graduation from high school, she worked to earn money so she could study at the Chicago Evangelistic Institute. The Institute was established in 1910 and was known throughout the United States and Canada as a non-denominational school with an emphasis on social action. Women as well as men were encouraged to enroll in this school of theology.

My parents met at the Institute. Mom said she first became aware of Harold Sherk when she and some friends gathered together before a church service. She would lead several women down the aisle to the pew she chose. Shortly thereafter, several young men led by Harold Sherk would enter the pew at the other end. Dad would sit beside Mom and share a hymnbook with her.

I don't think either of my parents finished studies at CEI. Dad returned to Ontario to respond to his call to the ministry. Mom returned to New Jersey to earn money to finish her preparation for the mission field.

But Dad had other ideas. He wrote to Mom asking her to marry him. She didn't answer immediately. After a week or two she accepted his proposal. She laughed as she remembered a comment that her brother made as she packed her bag and traveled alone out of the country to marry a stranger he, Elwood, had never met: "At least he could have come and escorted you to your new home." They were married on October 16, 1926 at a service held in the living room of the old farmhouse where Dad was born.

Mom thought she and Dad would be missionaries to Africa, but then she became pregnant and that changed everything. She would not raise a child in Africa; there was too much illness and too few doctors and nurses.

Iva Ruth Sherk was born on May 6, 1928. Mom remembered how busy she was with one baby. She laughed as she told me the story of the time Dad came home to his wife and new baby after an afternoon of visiting parishioners, and asked whether she had eaten anything. "I had an eggnog," she said. "Couldn't you at least cook the egg?" he asked.

John Harold Sherk, Junior was born March 6, 1931, and Frank Arthur Sherk on May 20, 1932. Mildred Lillian Sherk made a disruptive entrance at the worst possible time for all concerned, on Sunday morning, January 26, 1936, in a blizzard. The doctor could not make it through the storm on time for the delivery, and Dad had to call his intern—a helper, they were called then—who made it through the blizzard to the church to preach the sermon.

My siblings had brown hair and brown eyes like Mom. Dad was fair with light brown hair and blue eyes. My hair was blonde—"a towhead," my mother said. My eyes were blue, and mom said that people, on meeting our family, always assumed I was adopted. I was distressed by what I considered a negative assessment. So was Iva, who was tired of hearing about her little sister's blonde hair. "You would have thought the rest of us were bald," she said.

As a young pastor's wife during the Depression, my mother received many gifts of food for her family. There was little money, but farmers brought vegetables from their gardens and fruit from their orchards. When the farmers butchered an animal, the meat was tithed and ten per cent was given to the pastor and his family. When sheep were sheared, ten per cent of the wool was given to the pastor. Sometimes recipes accompanied the gifts of food. Mom learned to can meat. During the Depression our family ate well.

There was another source of meat for the family. Dad had grown up on a farm and was expert in the use of his rifle. Iva recalled that sometimes at night, when the moon was full, Dad propped a bedroom window open a few inches. In the garden, he had piled several leaves of green lettuce on the mulch. In the middle of the night Iva would hear the crack of a rifle, and she knew that rabbit was on the menu that evening.

I don't think we appreciated the fact that Mom was living in different culture from the one she was born and grew up in. She was living in a foreign land, and her family was her husband's people whose first language, Pennsylvania Dutch, she did not understand. Her children learned games and songs she did not know in a language she did not speak. She'd moved from her small birth family to a large extended family, without her mother close by. In one setting a motherly neighbor provided great support; in the other an irate parishioner agitated an entire congregation.

An older gentleman in one congregation did not agree with my Dad's theology, and actively worked to undermine his ministry. Mom watched her husband agonize over how to deal with this threat to the ministry in this part of the church. The little rural community in southern Ontario had very traditional gender roles. Didn't the Bible say that women should not speak in the church, and if they had questions they should ask their husbands at home? But Mom had had enough. The next Sunday morning, she delivered the sermon. Decades later she could tell me the text on which her sermon was based. I can't remember it now, but it may be that the medium was the message. Decades later, when Mom told me this story, she made no apologies. She and Dad were a team in their ministry, and their two voices were one in harmony.

Mom was a fierce defender of her children. One afternoon a month the ladies gathered at the church and pieced and stitched a quilt that was sold to raise money for missions. The afternoons were spent in sewing and gossip. Mom calculated how much money she was making for missions with an afternoon of quilting. The next scheduled quilting day she carried a quarter in to the quilters and put it on the table. She explained that she had calculated how much money they received for a finished quilt, minus costs that were reimbursed, divided by the number of hours it took to make it, and determined that she earned a quarter for missions with an afternoon of quilting. She would not be coming to quilt for missions she told the group. She would send a quarter in and spend the time with her children, who needed her care and nurturance. One of the ladies responded: "Well Mila, you always were a strange one."

II

Both of my parents were radical Christians. By that I mean that they tried to understand how Jesus' message, particularly the Sermon on the Mount in The Gospel of Matthew, should be reflected in their daily lives. I was three years old when World War II began. Dad was brought up in the Mennonite Brethren in Christ Church, one of the 22 varieties of Mennonites. Our Mennonites emphasized evangelism, but not pacifism. When the war began, Mom told me, Dad puzzled over what he should be teaching and preaching, and how he should be living. "You know your Dad lived an integrated life," Mom said, "and as he studied the Sermon on the Mount and Mennonite doctrine, he came to the conclusion that Jesus taught peacemaking, and that's where his energy should go."

And it did. At a time when pacifism was despised, Dad became secretary of the Ontario conference of Historic Peace Churches, a group of Quaker, Brethren in Christ, and Mennonite church leaders. He and other pastors lobbied the government in Ottawa for recognition of conscientious objectors (CO's) in Canada. After this alternative was recognized, he became a chaplain to the CO men in work camps, living in a tent in the winter as they did.

That was the winter of 1942. The tents in the camp were kept as warm as possible with gas heaters. The heater in Dad's tent started a fire, and the tent and all of the books he had taken with him, including two volumes of Henry's Bible, a beloved New Testament commentary, were destroyed. Dad continued to serve as chaplain until mom became very ill. She had a high fever and became delirious, and Dad had to return home to care for his wife and family. I remember one evening before Dad had come home from the western provinces, Mom started calling out to him. We four children were seated around the dining table, eating whatever the ladies in the local congregation had brought for our family that day. When Mom called out in a shrill voice to an unseen person in her room, Harold and Arthur followed their older sister's action and knelt beside their chairs and prayed quietly for their mother. I slipped out of my chair, knelt beside it, laid my head on my arms and cried.

I think it was during the time that Dad was gone that Mom instituted family circle. At nine in the evening, no matter what we were doing, we put our work down and gathered in the living room. We sang a hymn, read some scripture, and a parent prayed before we went to bed.

After Dad returned to the family and Mom recovered, he became involved in establishing an institute for the training of pastors in our denomination in Ontario. The following year he filled a pastoral vacancy in Markham, Ontario. Then he continued developing the curriculum and teaching courses at Emmanuel Bible College, which had moved to Kitchener.

At that time our family moved to the farm where Dad had been born and his parents still lived, which was three miles from Kitchener. My grandparents lived in the main part of the big old farmhouse; our family lived in an extension that had been built for Grandma Sherk's parents, "the doddy house." We were told that Dad, who was two or three years old when the extension was being built, had once scared all of the grownups by climbing up a ladder that was leaning against the roof.

III

Two or three years after our family moved to our grandparents' farm, when we were on the way home from church one Sunday morning, Dad steered the car over to the side of the road and stopped. Mom was very quiet as Dad said to us: "What would you think if I were to go to India for two years?" Eleven-year-old Arthur began to sing: "Goodbye, Pharaoh, Goodbye." We laughed together. Dad told us more about details of what he believed he was being called to do. He told us that there were great floods in India. Many people had lost their homes and family; many lost their lives. There was great poverty, hunger, and widespread illness. But food and hospital supplies had been donated from Mennonite communities all over North America, and they needed someone to see that those supplies reached the people who needed them. Dad would oversee others in the Mennonite Central Committee (MCC), a relief organization of all the Mennonite churches in Canada and the United States. (At this time India was still under the rule of Great Britain, and the sub-continent had not yet been divided into Hindu and Muslim states.) Sitting in the car with my parents and siblings, it was clear to me that once again we needed to share our Dad. I don't recall anyone expressing reluctance or negativity.

I do remember that on the day that Dad left for India, he, Mom, and Iva left the farmhouse and I was alone with my brothers. The plan was for Iva, 16 years old with a new driver's license, to drive our parents to the train station in Hamilton. (Iva would be the family driver while Dad was in India; Mom never drove.) Mom would go on with Dad to Pennsylvania for a week of orientation. Then Dad was to get on a ship for a long journey to India and Mom would return home to her children. I was eight years old. I stood in the dining room, by the door that had closed behind my sister and parents, and cried. Arthur put his arm around my shoulder and said: "Don't cry, In a few hours Iva will be home, and then in one week Mom will be home, and then in two years Dad will be home, and we will all be together again." I felt comforted.

During the time Dad was in India, Mom shouldered whatever responsibilities were necessary. She taught us that Dad had been called to this service, and we should support him and God would take care of all of us. Her ministry was a quiet one in the home, one that occupied all of her energies, and I can't say that I ever felt anxious about Dad's absence, although we all missed him very much.

While he was in India, once a week we received a letter journaling his activities. We gathered together to hear Mom read them to us. On our birthday for two years we children got individual letters from Dad. His last months in India were in dangerous times. Dad wrote of being surrounded by a mob who tried to drag him out of a taxi in Calcutta. Wherever he went he took his 8mm movie camera with him, documenting first the ministry of some of the historic peace churches in World War II and then the relief services of the Mennonite Church in India around the time of the Indian struggle for independence. I think Dad's movies and writing from this time are in the Conrad Grebel College archives in Waterloo, Ontario.

It was while Dad was in India that the Ontario school system decided to screen all children for exposure to tuberculosis. We came home with positive skin tests, and I remember my mother and her four children soberly walking down the road to a sanatorium about two miles from our home to have chest x-rays. Her own mother had several brothers who'd contracted tuberculosis and were cared for in her home when Mom was three years old. The shadow of tuberculosis followed her throughout her life. But, although we had strong positive skin tests, none of us had radiographic evidence of tuberculosis infection, and no treatment was given.

On his return to Canada, Dad didn't have an assignment, and that summer our family's income was limited. We lived on Grandpa's farm and raised the food we ate. The large garden provided vegetables, the old fruit vines and trees provided fruit, and the flock of chickens provided eggs and meat. After a period of time, Dad was assigned to teach at Emmanuel Bible College again.

IV

In 1949 Dad accepted a position as Secretary of the Peace Section at the MCC headquarters in Akron, Pennsylvania. The three oldest children were settled into independent housing: my sister Iva studied medicine in Toronto, and my two brothers, Harold and Arthur, lived together in the Thaler family home in Kitchener. Iva became a pathologist, and head of a regional laboratory in southern Ontario. Harold fell in love with the Thalers' youngest daughter, Ruth, and established a business as a watchmaker. Mid-career he returned to school and entered the ministry. Arthur travelled to Hamilton to study undergraduate mathematics at McMaster University and went on to graduate work in solid geometry at the University of Toronto. He was a professor of geometry at the university until he retired in 1994.

In Pennsylvania with my parents, I began grade ten in Ephrata High School, graduating in 1952. I was two years younger than my classmates, and so I worked for two years in the MCC organization as a telephone operator and a mail clerk. In 1954, a few months before I entered college, Mom was hospitalized with hemoptysis. An active tubercular lung infection was found. She had lost more than one third of normal lung function. She was transferred to a tuberculosis sanitarium in southern Ontario, where she was hospitalized for a year and a half.

When it was time for me to go to college, Dad packed me and my big trunk into his Oldsmobile (he always bought second-hand Oldsmobile sedans or wagons) and we struck out for northern Indiana. Dad continued to work as head of the

Peace Section of the MCC, where his work was to interface with churches and individuals who wanted to learn more about the pacifist position and might need support as they came before their local draft board for classification as conscientious objectors to war.

After ten years in the little village of Akron, Pennsylvania, my parents moved to Washington, D.C., where Dad continued his work in peacemaking as Executive Secretary of the multidenominational National Service Board for Religious Objectors to War. They purchased the first and only home they ever owned, in Prince George's County. The war in Vietnam had begun, and public sentiment was moving toward recognition of the validity of conscientious objection that wasn't based on a particular strand of religious thought.

During his ten years at the national level, Dad worked to maintain healthy relationships with authorities in Selective Service. General Lewis B. Hershey had been appointed head of Selective

Service in 1941 and served for thirty years. Dad visited General Hershey when he was hospitalized, and General Hershey introduced Dad to his military colleagues as his personal chaplain. Both men seemed to hold the other in high regard, and when his health improved General Hershey and his wife were entertained for dinner in my parents' home in the Maryland suburbs of Washington. My mother received a thoughtful letter of condolence from General Hershey when my father died.

Dad had begun to have atrial fibrillation, and, since he was approaching age sixty-five, he retired, and he and Mom returned to Ontario. He had some cardiovascular difficulties and was hospitalized in Kitchener. I flew to Ontario with my three-year-old daughter, Mary Elizabeth. Mary, who was generally easygoing, had a major reaction in the center of the lobby of the hospital: she threw herself on the marble floor and beat her head and fists against it. We found a quiet place for her and my mother waited with her while I went to see Dad.

When I walked into Dad's hospital room he said, quietly, "I want to go home." I said, "You are home, Dad." He said, "No, I mean Waterloo County." I explained that he was in Waterloo County, and I had come from Baltimore to visit him. He looked puzzled and then fell asleep again. His health continued to fade and he died at age 70.

Mom lived to be 82, but with Dad's death she felt her work was done, and she wondered why God was keeping her around. Toward the end of her life, Mom told me that there were two principles she'd lived by in raising her children: one was to treat all the children the same; the second was to bring the first child up right, and that child then helps to bring up the others. I know Mom modified those principles to fit the occasion. She tried to provide similar advantages for each child in the family. At the same time, the plan to have the oldest child keep order in the ranks of the younger children did not have the desired results. You might say that Harold and Arthur and I were conscientious objectors to conscription into that movement.

Iva was busy with plans for her future. She studied constantly. There was a shortage of physicians in Canada post-World War II; Iva wanted to enroll in a six-year medical program that was developed at the University of Toronto. Somewhere around 200 students were accepted into the program—all men. It was two weeks before the program began that Iva and I think six other women were accepted.

My brothers were usually assigned a chore as a team by Mom or Dad or Grandpa, and developed their routines together. After my assignment at home was done I would find a book and disappear with it. My best hours were spent sitting on the roof of the smoke house in autumn, eating the grapes that grew up the side of the building and reading.

The determinant of equilibrium in our family was the strong faith of our parents. Dad, as the firstborn male child of nine (seven of whom survived to adulthood) born to Hubert and Lydia Troxel Sherk, was "given to God," much as the boy Samuel in the story in the Hebrew Bible was brought to the temple and given to God. Hubert and Lydia continued to play a major supporting role in their son's ministry by providing a home for his family. My brothers and I remember life on the farm as a happy time.

The story of this gift to God, however, cannot be told in isolation. It is not just the story of Harold Sherk, but of a family. This collection of Mom's stories tells some of her part in the family story. She reached the end of her life feeling, as we all did, that she had completed her assignment. She was determined to be content wherever she found herself, and she found herself raising four active, inquiring children, under unusual circumstances, sometimes with her life companion on the other side of the world. We felt secure because she was in charge. And she was content in raising us.

My fondest memories are of Mom at home, singing. She had a beautiful soprano voice, and I can still hear her solos in Sunday evening services, and the songs she sang as she dusted the furniture, or ironed the clothes: *"I sing because I'm happy. I sing because I'm free. For His eye is on the sparrow and I know He watches me."*

SUBTRACTION

My friends are quiet.

We sit at the table after dinner.
I tell them
I sent last month's rent late.

When the bill came this month
I couldn't subtract
What I'd already sent
To determine what I owed.

I remember
The two-room school
In Centreville
Where I learned to subtract.

I sat with other students in a fifth grade row,
Alphabetically.
Don't forget to borrow
Mrs. MacLean said.

If I break it down
to little steps
I can learn again.
It's not difficult.

I have 21 bricks.
How many bricks will I have
if I give you 13?
Eight, I think.

If I have 217 ice cream cones

and eat 130 of them, what is left?

I would say some melted ice cream

and a bellyache.

What is 53721 minus 53109?

Beats me.

I haven't forgotten.

I understand the problem but

I cannot complete the steps.

How can I borrow melted ice cream?

A PEARL HARBOR SURVIVOR

It is Thursday morning, quarter after five. The local news is on television. Next is a story about a Pearl Harbor survivor: a California man serenaded by twenty sailors on his ninety-eighth birthday.

I reflected on the thoughts we are told returning military men have—*why did I survive when my friends didn't*—and the thought popped into my head, *I am a survivor of sorts,* because I have had experiences that have taken the lives of others.

In 1958 I was driving six nursing graduates from northern Indiana to Indianapolis to take nursing board exams. Directly ahead in my lane at the crest of a hill, a tractor-trailer suddenly appeared. In a half a heartbeat I swerved to the shoulder of the road and we safely continued on our way. I kept driving. No one spoke for a long time. In fact, no one who was in that car ever talked with me about that experience.

One time, years ago, I entered the main building of the Enoch Pratt Free Library and decided to take the elevator instead of walking up a flight of stairs. As I approached the elevator, one man who had a payphone receiver to his ear nodded to another man and hung up the phone. Both men got on my elevator. I immediately pushed the open button; the door opened and I got out. For some unknown reason I raced up the stairs to see where they'd gone, but they were nowhere to be seen.

And then there was my experience in the remote parking lot at the Philadelphia Airport. It was quite some time before I could talk about that. In 1990 Sid, Mary Elizabeth, and I took a cruise up the inner passage to Alaska. Tim was finishing a summer job. Our air passage home from the west coast was cancelled: that weekend President George H. W. Bush needed the passenger planes to move troops in Desert Storm. Sid, who was scheduled for major surgery at Johns Hopkins Hospital the next day, found a flight for himself, and one Mary Elizabeth so she could stay overnight at a hotel that was across the street from Hopkins.

The flight he found for me was several hours later and I arrived in Philadelphia at ten o'clock at night instead of mid-afternoon. Our car was in the remote parking area. I knew the bus stop I needed, but didn't remember the exact place I'd parked the car in relation to the bus stop.

When I got out of the bus, I smelled tobacco— good, rich pipe tobacco. That concerned me, because there was no one to be seen. I started across the parking lot but couldn't find my car, so

I walked quickly back to the lighted bus stop and got inside in the light. I turned and saw a tall man standing with his back to me just outside the door. He was in a torn sweater that had originally been of very good quality. He was slender and athletic. I was sure he was up to no good.

I said quietly: Look God, my family isn't going to handle this well. Do something fast. And just then two cars pulled up to where we were standing and stopped. Their headlights lighted a path across the road and I picked up my suitcase and walked out. But I thought, *this guy is just going to wait for another woman to come along... I have to scare him...* and I stood and turned and looked at the man by the door. His face was in a shadow, and I couldn't see it, but I stared like I was trying to remember his features. Then I quickly turned and walked ahead a little farther, and there was my car. I had my key in my hand, unlocked the car, threw my suitcase in and got in. I looked back to the bus stop. There was no one there. I locked the car and drove away. My husband was alone in a hospital and my daughter was alone in a hotel room across the street from him. I had to get to Baltimore.

I BELONG

In 1955 there was a photography exhibition at the Museum of Modern Art in New York. Edward Steichen wrote: "'The Family of Man' was conceived of as a mirror of the universal elements in the everydayness of life." In the Prologue to the exhibition catalogue, Carl Sandburg wrote: "The first cry of a baby in Chicago, or Zambounge, in Amsterdam or Rangoon, has the same pitch and key, each saying, 'I am! I have come through! I belong! I am a member of the family!'"

After seven years of marriage, Sid and I had reached several milestones. He had completed undergraduate study for a Bachelor of Arts degree with a major in English, all of the required work for entry into medical school, and one year of post-graduate work at Ohio State University while he applied for entrance to a medical school. He received a doctor of medicine degree from Wake Forest University in June of 1965. He was accepted into an internship and residency program, located at the old Baltimore City hospital, now the Bayview campus of Johns Hopkins Hospital.

In his last year of medical school we started thinking about having a family. Sid and I each had an older sister who had an adopted child, and we thought it would be fine if one of our children was adopted, so there would be a network of adopted children in the family. We began adoption procedures.

The first time I held Tim he was about seven weeks old. Our social worker at the adoption agency thought this baby was a good match with us. I was so focused on the baby, whom we called Timothy, that he's all I remember from that visit. I honestly   cannot remember whether anyone else was in the room. I do remember I was told to sit in a chair and a baby was placed in my arms. I looked at the baby a long time, and he studied my face. I knew his gaze was an indication of normal brain development and nothing more, but it pleased me that he was so alert, and I was glad it was my face that he was learning to know. I'd been reflecting on the power that was being exerted over this baby simply because he was being adopted, and I apologized to him for all the life-changing decisions that were being made for him without any input from him. I remember saying that, as much as possible, I would involve him in decision-making about himself. Several days later Sidney and I took Timmy home to our apartment on the grounds of Baltimore City Hospital.

Timmy had been in our home for less than a month when Sid and I were at dinner with several faculty members and their wives. Psychiatrist Dr. Jerome Frank was seated beside me, and he asked, "Do you have children?"

"Yes, " I said, "a little boy, Timothy." Wishing to be straightforward, I added, "He's adopted."

"Oh, but he's yours! " Dr. Frank said immediately. I realized that I had said he was adopted as if that were the most important fact about him. What mattered was that he belonged.

When Timmy was eight months old, a doctoral student at Johns Hopkins University phoned and said she was studying maternal infant attachment behaviors under the direction of a Dr. Mary Ainsworth. She said she'd been given my name by our pediatrician. She explained the study to me and wondered whether I'd be willing for Timmy to be included in it. After I was sure that she understood I was an adoptive mother and that, although I was the primary caregiver, I taught nursing part time and we did have a part-time babysitter, I was delighted to agree to Timmy's participation in the study. Timmy was also delighted. Several times, both in our apartment and in a room at the university, an attractive young woman came and played with him. She brought the most interesting toys with her. I remember a ball with a transparent cover, in the center of which a butterfly with shimmering wings was suspended from a fine cord. As I remember it, when the ball was rolled, the butterfly would wind up; when the ball stopped rolling, the butterfly in the ball unwound. It was visually captivating.

When Timmy was two and a half years old, we moved to a split-level brick home in a development in Harford County. It was a difficult move for him. Home had changed radically and Timmy became very restless. He stopped taking naps. We decided to postpone adoption of a second child for a while.

Timmy and I read a lot of children's books together, and talked about the pictures. We went to the public library in Bel Air for story time, and he picked out books to read at home. Somewhere along the way to the library he found comic books and couldn't get enough of them. Every word had to be read, including the ZAPS!!! and POWS!!!.

It was around that same time that *Sesame Street* began on public television. Timmy loved to watch *Sesame Street*. He learned numbers and letters. He enjoyed the conversations and music. He also watched *Captain Chesapeake* and sometimes *Mister Roger's Neighborhood*. We borrowed Illustrated children's books from the library and purchased many for Timmy's bookshelf. I wouldn't read comic books to him—I couldn't see that they made a positive contribution to his education—and told him he would have to read them himself. He was up to the challenge, and he was reading comic books in kindergarten. At age six he had a small, select collection of comic books that was the envy of the high school kids at church when we had a picnic for them.

When he was three, he was enrolled in Trinity Lutheran Preschool. Sid and I felt that Tim needed to be around other children. He lived in a grownup world and handled himself very well there, but how would he relate to other children? He quickly formed a close friendship with the three-year-old son of a local mortician. Tim and Howard K. took over and ran a tight play yard for a very short period of time, until the teachers saw what was happening..

When Tim settled down in our new home, we contacted Family and Children's Society and began the adoption procedure for a second child. A social worker made the usual home visit as part of the adoption process for Mary Elizabeth. Timmy was an articulate three-year-old who carried on a conversation about many things and totally blew her away.

We brought Mary Elizabeth home when she was five weeks old. A medical resident's work at

Baltimore City Hospitals was demanding, and Sidney was unable to accompany the family when Tim and I, together with Peternel, our Dutch au pair, went to Family and Children's Society to bring a tiny Mary Elizabeth home. It was Labor Day weekend, and Peternel went to an MCC-sponsored gathering. Sidney, Tim, Mary Elizabeth and I went to Chincoteague for the weekend, a first family outing. It was very hot, and we spent the weekend in the air-conditioned motel room and went home early.

Again there was a brief introductory period where we got used to each other's presence, but very quickly I felt a bond: *This child is our child.* I knew that others had brought the baby to the place where she could join our family, and I was grateful for that.

Mary Elizabeth was a quiet baby. She was a "watcher." And in her brother she found a lot to watch. Tim was her favorite entertainment. He bounced around her inventing stories that included her. Everything he did seemed to interest her. I watched the two of them to make sure the activities didn't disadvantage her. She grew up to be an observant, active, tolerant participant in her brother's games; a favorite was "Rabbit Country." Tim pronounced his sister "a good playmate." As I watched each child grow and develop, I knew that they belonged in our family. I wanted them to know how dear they are to Sid and me.

We had a cat who was known by several different names. She was a kitten when we moved to the farm, and lived to be around eighteen years of age. The children and I loved her, but Sid barely tolerated her. "She makes no positive contribution to the farm," he said. We begged to differ. She didn't create problems. She did sleep with her head under the woodstove when there was a hot fire inside, which made us question how bright she was. But she could catch any mouse that was so foolhardy as to come into a room she was in.

Outside the home Mary Elizabeth was very shy. We enrolled her in morning preschool at age three because she needed to learn other social behaviors. But she still watched what went on around her. She didn't seek leadership in class activities; she was content to watch others. She noticed children who seemed to be on the fringes and tried to befriend them, but if they became too attached to her, she sought adult help to make some personal space.

When Tim had completed grade two and Mary Elizabeth had completed her second year of preschool, we bought a 70-acre farm with an old stone farm house in Churchville, near the geographic center of Harford County. In the basement there was a kitchen fireplace that bore the date 1803 on the hearth. The old house had had very few changes since it was built. There was a bathroom with an old Victorian claw bathtub on the second floor, and a small powder room by the back door on the first floor. The kitchen in the basement was no longer used for cooking. An addition to the house several decades after it was first constructed built a kitchen, complete with a functioning fireplace, on the first floor.

We moved to the old farm before Mary Elizabeth started grade one and Tim was to begin grade four. At the end of grade one, Mary's teacher said: "She is so shy... how will she ever get on in the world?" I didn't worry about her. I knew how tough she was, because I had already tried to get her to do things she didn't want to do. I knew she had uncommon common sense and would progress through life without a lot of hoopla.

She had a way of going right to the heart of a matter. One Sunday morning when she was five years old, her church schoolteacher came to me and said, "I asked the children this morning what a mother does. The children said things like she cleans the house and she cooks food for you to eat. Mary Elizabeth laughed. 'You can pay somebody to do that,' she told the class. She said. 'Mothers love you.'"

A few years later she came steaming out of her Sunday school class; her teacher had told her that her ideas were heresy. Obviously she had asked some question that he didn't like. But I assured her that God was not going to damn her because she was asking questions that were not part of a given denomination's theology.

Years later, as I was studying in an ecumenical graduate school, I was challenged by a viewpoint the teacher expressed and I thought: What is true for my daughter is true for me. I can explore and ask questions and think thoughts outside the pale established by a denomination. A God of love is not going to cut me down for such questions. Throughout our life together, my children have taught me how to grow.

I asked both Tim and Mary to write down things they remembered from their childhood. Tim gave me a six-page list. Mary said, "You don't really expect me to do that, do you?" Then she read Tim's list and laughed: *I remember this... I remember this...*

Some things he remembered:

Family hugs, where Mom and Dad would lift Mary and me up to grownup altitude for a big group embrace.

I went through a finicky spell sometime in my childhood where I would eat fewer and fewer foods, until I would eat only peanut butter sandwiches until finally I didn't like them any more and would eat nothing. Mom broke this logjam by making me green eggs and ham, using food coloring. As I recall I was so amazed that Mom had done something so whimsical and strange that I ate them. Plus, if you've read Green Eggs and Ham *and internalized its lesson, it's hard to refuse to eat actual green eggs and ham when they are presented to you.*

I remember watching TV in the family room downstairs at Green Spring. We would

cancel all plans and gather round the televi-
sion with a bowl of popcorn for yearly air-
ings of the Charlie Brown specials and The
Wizard of Oz. *Later on Mom and I watched*
Blazing Saddles, Murder by Death *and* Foul
Play. [Clevon Little, in *Blazing Saddles*, was
the first actor I saw who mocked white ig-
norance with his portrayal of a black sheriff, and he delighted me.]

Tim continued:

Not too long after we saw Blazing Saddles, *someone with a British accent called*
and gave Mom the message that "a dozen
black mockers" (markers) had arrived for
Dad. Mom did not look forward to the arri-
val of these men.

I remember Mom reading us Anne of
Green Gables *out loud by Coleman lamp-*
light in the pop-up camper on a trip to the

maritime provinces, and all of us weeping
when sweet old Matthew Cuthbert died.

Dad was always sneakily trying to cir-
cumvent my natural laziness and get me to
do ambitious academic stuff. He enrolled us
both in classes at Hopkins in the summer:
astronomy and music history. [Sid told me
that Tim's course grade was higher than
his.]

Adoptive families are minority families. It
was important to Sid and me that our children
feel secure, belonging where they found them-
selves. Casual conversations could make them
feel different. One time in the car when she was
six or seven, Mary Elizabeth popped out the
question, "Why didn't my parents want me?" I
said the first thing that came into my mind:
"They didn't know you. They only knew that they
were going to have a baby. They didn't even
know if it would be a boy or a girl. But they knew
they couldn't give the baby a good home, and

they wanted the baby to have a good home." The answer satisfied her, and she never brought the subject up again.

Tim kept his own counsel. As he grew up he read. Almost every book that he saw he picked up and read. And he loved to draw. If you wanted to know what he was thinking about you looked at his pictures.

Tim and Mary E. and I went to see old movies like *The Cabinet of Dr. Caligari* that were shown at the Enoch Pratt library. In summer both children went to programs offered by Maryland Institute, College of Art.

Tim writes in one of his books about his elementary school playmates. He seldom made comments at home about the game of "defriending" that the boys in elementary school engaged in, but I didn't like it. I remembered a similar game played in the little country school I attended as a child in Ontario, and I found nothing to commend it.

Tim had big ideas about making movies, and he wrote stories and filmed his friends. Sidney learned that Johns Hopkins University was starting a program for gifted children, and encouraged Tim to participate. Tim wanted to get involved in the writing seminar program. Both children attended the Center for Academically Talented Youth as students, and continued as staff. By the time he entered Hopkins's undergraduate writing program, Tim had accumulated enough credits to enter at a sophomore level.

As Mary Elizabeth grew up, I found it difficult to assess her cognitive strengths and interests. She was quiet. She enjoyed the company of other children, but didn't talk about her interests and activities at home. It was when she was fifteen years old and we shared a small apartment in Switzerland for a year that I saw how bright she was. She was admitted to the International School of Geneva, eleventh grade. Her classmates were from countries around the world. Their parents were employed in international organizations. They had been educated in private international schools; Mary Elizabeth had been educated in Harford County public schools. But she was attentive in class. At home she required no reminders to do any work that she had been assigned. When she did her homework, she concentrated on the work to be done and completed it rapidly. At the end of the year she ranked third in a class of 120 students at the school. I decided she had the cognitive tools to be successful in life. When she graduated from the University of Pennsylvania Medical School, I sent her picture in to *The Aegis*, the Harford County paper, hoping that her first-grade teacher would see it.

Tim and Mary hold some values in common, but they are very different. As they grew up I didn't try to compare them. Mr. Rogers and I liked them just the way they are. We had competitions, but there were categories: Tim always won in one category—for example, six-year-old boys with brown hair—and Mary E in another—three-year-old girls with braids.

Tim is now a writer; Mary Elizabeth is a physician. But they are so much more than what they do. And I know that they are God's greatest gifts to Sidney and to me. For our beloved children, my prayer is that they care for others and walk in safety; that they love beauty and graciousness; that they live each day grounded in the knowledge that they are an essential part of the world they live in. That they belong.

THE MAN WHO SAVED MY LIFE

Six years ago I almost lost my life. I was living alone on my farm in an old stone house built when Thomas Jefferson was president. The restoration of the house was complete, and I enjoyed having relatives and friends come to see the changes. The geothermal heating and cooling unit I had installed made the old place incredibly comfortable. The restored fireplace in the kitchen was fun to cook in. We discovered, when we took up the brick floor in the basement, that two hundred years ago, when they were making brick, the family dog had stepped into a soft brick. His misadventure was recorded for posterity. After the brick had hardened it was turned over and used in the floor beside the cooking hearth. When we discovered it we thought about the family who'd lived on the farm two hundred years ago. And we wondered what the farm would look like in two hundred years more.

One day In April, 2010 I thought I had the flu. My muscles ached, I felt feverish, my head ached, and I was very tired. I should have gone to bed, but I had another piece of land with an old stone farmhouse to rent. So I drove twenty minutes on back roads to the old house, called Mt Pleasant. When I got there, I waited for the potential renters, but felt so miserable that when they arrived I just handed them the key and told them to look at the old house and grounds and pass the key on to my nephew. I drove home, barely able to pay attention to the road.

When I got home I had a call from my potential renters. They reported that someone had broken into the house, drained the propane from the tank, cut out the copper pipes and generally trashed the place.

I thought I knew who it was. A contractor had made at least two visits to the old farm recently, saying he wanted to buy the place for his family. Something didn't ring true in his story. When he brought his wife to see the farmhouse, it was clear that she had no real interest in it.

At home, I decided to call the sheriff's office. My nephew said it would do no good, but at least the incident would be recorded in the Sheriff's office. The man who answered the phone indicated they were too busy to talk with me then, but they would send a deputy to my home in the evening to get my report.

When the deputy arrived that evening there was no answer to his knock. He looked inside and saw me lying unconscious on the floor. The next thing I knew I was being taken down our farm's lane in an ambulance to the emergency room of the new hospital in Bel Air. I remember saying, "Please don't use the siren. It will disturb my neighbors."

In the emergency room my blood pressure was read at 60/40. I was in septic shock. A large kidney stone had blocked my right ureter, and the right kidney was in early stages of hydronephrosis. I didn't have pain from that, but my throat was very sore, apparently from attempts to insert a large airway while I was unconscious.

I survived. I was hospitalized at Upper Chesapeake Health System for a week. It took two days before the medical team could find an antibiotic that could kill the infecting bacteria. The kidney stone was crushed in surgery. I survived atrial fibrillation, had my first experience of hallucinations, was transferred to Good Samaritan Hospital for rehabilitation, and decided maybe it was time to move off the farm.

But the idea I keep coming back to, even to this day, is that I was saved by the actions of a greedy man who took something of value that belonged to me, and unwittingly gave me my life in exchange. I'm not angry at him; I'm not grateful to him. I just know that simple notions of right and wrong are no longer enough. Over time I have learned that any action I take has the potential to do harm as well as good, no matter how noble my motivation. Now I know that the smallest gesture, the least passing moment, may have unexpected consequences: a pet's misstep is preserved for centuries; a man who sought to take advantage of me saved my life.

EVERY MAN IS AN ISLAND

Every man is an island

Stones and grains of sand
Loosened by tide and waves
And washed away.

Tonight I go to drawing class.
Study began fifty years past.
I can't remember many words but
I remember the images.

Ahead of me in the hall
Rob walks to dinner.
Pushing an empty wheelchair
He needs for support.

He stops to rest.
I catch up to him.
How are things? I ask.
Not so good, he replies.

I don't know what to say.
We need your song, I say.
I have the first four notes, he says.
Terrific, I say.

I think of Rob as I sit at my desk.
My art assignment unfinished.
My linoleum cutter unused.
I lack strength and dexterity.

Things are not so good.

My teacher says, hold it like this.

Take out what you want to have white.

The black will be negative space.

Negative space, that's me.

It's part of the image I am creating.

And negative space helps tell the story.

There is no story, no image, without nega-

tive space.

There is no island without water.

An Irreplaceable Loss

So long as men can breathe, or eyes can see,
So long lives this, and this gives life to thee.

-William Shakespeare, Sonnet XVIII

It was September, 1954. I was a freshman in a small liberal arts college in northern Indiana. Fall semester had begun. In the freshman women's dorm we were closing our books for the evening when we heard a sound outside. Rhythmic, harmonious, definitely male voices sang: "*Mr. Sandman, bring me a dream...*" We rushed out onto the third floor porch to see what was happening.

Beneath us on the campus green were the up-turned faces of twenty or so sophomore men. At the front was a young Greek god whose name was Sidney.

Apparently Sidney sat two rows behind me in a required course, "Introduction to Fine Arts," where our time was spent listening to classical music and looking at art masterpieces. The sophomore boys were looking at the freshman girls.

Sidney was the best-looking guy in the class. He had a beautiful tenor voice. He was funny and smart, had an exceptional wardrobe, and, believe it or not, he liked me!

Four years later, after graduation from college, we began a marriage that lasted thirty-three years—a significant amount of time then, but, twenty-five years later, seems far too short.

Sidney was health-conscious: he was very active, walked a lot, used stairs rather than elevators, kept his weight at healthy levels, watched his diet, took screening tests. When we first learned that he had a diagnosis of cancer of the colon, it seemed unreal. But the evidence confirmed the diagnosis.

Our first concern was for our children. The prognosis was not good, but there was hope. Sidney was determined to live, and when he died five years later, he had exhausted all possibilities of treatment.

July 26, 1991 was Sidney's birthday, his fifty-sixth, and Mary Elizabeth's, her twenty-first. I think there were eight close family friends who came that evening to celebrate Mary Elizabeth's birthday with our family. There was talking and four-part singing and an ice cream birthday cake downstairs. Upstairs Sidney and I listened to the music. One at a time our Presbyterian pastor Gus, Tim, and Mary Elizabeth came upstairs to tell us what was happening downstairs, and listened to Sidney's last words to them.

Sidney thought he could will himself to die, but the life force was strong in him, and it wasn't until a week later, Friday, August 2, at three in the morning, that he breathed his last. The following Monday morning there was a private burial service for family and closest friends. I have memories of a funeral procession that started on the farm where we lived and followed the centuries-old dirt road along Deer Creek to Deer Creek Harmony Church. Tim sat in the hearse to lead the procession through the maze of roads that his father loved. I was sure we were going to get lost and end up driving to Conowingo Dam or some such place. I should have known better.

Monday evening there was a memorial service. The church was filled to overflowing. Mary Elizabeth couldn't find the belt to her dress. Who cares, we wondered. Sidney had planned the service himself: there were four pastors and a barbershop quartet. Each pastor had played a special role in our family's history, and Sidney loved barbershop close harmony. He'd been a second tenor. His high school voice teacher said that he really was a baritone, but choir directors would probably make him a tenor because, as my brother Arthur said, they were as scarce as hen's teeth.

We got through Thanksgiving Day. We went to visit Sidney's sister and her family in Pennsylvania. When we got home that evening, Tim and Mary and I gathered around the wood stove in the kitchen. The house was cold. The fire we started in the stove began to warm up the kitchen. I said, "I'm tired of this," and Tim said, "Yeah, it's not funny anymore, Dad." We sipped cocoa in a kitchen that was warming up, then went to bed, because that's what you do when Thanksgiving Day is over. Life would continue without Sidney, and I knew that my children would have to engage in the usual activities of people in their early twenties, and that I needed to help them keep moving along.

I remember two things from that time. I felt like I was circling around a great black hole. I was afraid to cry, fearful that if I started I could never stop—I would be sucked into that great black hole. And I remember how incredibly supportive my children were. So many people around us seemed unaware of the deep grief that our family felt. Mary Elizabeth said gently: "Mom, maybe we are expecting too much."

Sidney had said don't forget me, and ordered forget-me-not seeds. Every spring I planted forget-me-not seeds or plants at the farm. Some of them grew, but I never really established a sturdy stand of forget-me-nots.

At the University School of Nursing I was assigned to be department chair of a community-oriented department that had community health, psychiatric and adult primary care nursing courses and programs. The dean wanted my department to establish a community-based nurse managed clinic in west Baltimore. I wrote a grant that provided funding for the beginning of a nurse-managed clinic in West Baltimore for three years. On two occasions, when the Department of Maternal Child Nursing was without a chair, I served as Acting Chair of that Department. My schedule was very full, but I wanted to be busy. The Dean of the School of Nursing at that time was a hardworking visionary who set the bar high for School of Nursing faculty. She was most supportive of me and my department, and I tried to reward her vote of confidence in me with my best efforts. I tried to provide an environment where faculty could do their best work. Desktop computers were introduced to the School of Nursing faculty, and we immediately moved into high gear. There was no time to grieve; there was too much work to be done.

Then, a year after Sidney's death, I talked on the telephone with a professor who was on a doctoral dissertation committee that I chaired. His voice reminded me of Sidney's voice, and when I hung up the telephone I started to cry. For the next four years I taught and ran one or two departments during the day and cried at night. I kept hearing the widow's song in Mendelssohn's Oratorio, *The Elijah*, in which the widow begs Elijah to return her son to life:

I go mourning all the day long, I lie down and weep at night. See my affliction. Be thou the orphan's helper...

I remember playing the *Elijah* over and over, especially the widow's song and Elijah's prayer, the section closing with the chorus: *"Blessed are the men who fear Him; they ever walk in the ways of peace. "*

I became hypertensive and had visual problems. My internist tried several combinations of medications, but my blood pressure did not stabilize in a therapeutic range until I retired from the university. And when my ophthalmologist examined my eyes, he commented that the corneas were boggy. I thought, I'm crying so much I am ruining my eyes. There are things worse than the death of your husband: being blind and being a widow, for example. I stopped crying immediately.

I had a professional gardener design flower gardens around the house and yard, and I asked him to include forget-me-not plants in the design. When the farm was sold there was a patch of forget-me-not plants thriving in the back yard, beside the little stone building once used as a slave's quarters.

IS GOD REAL?

"Grammy," asked six-year-old Lucas, "is Santa Claus real?"

I paused. In the Hebrew day care center where my grandchildren Lucas and Sydney were lovingly taught tolerance and respect for others, each child told her classmates of the December religious celebration in her family. Lucas and Sydney and their parents celebrated the Christmas season. That year, as Sydney greeted friends and relatives, her first question was "Are you Christian or Jewish?", and she shared what she learned about celebration of Hanukkah and Christmas.

Lucas and Sydney and their parents celebrate the Christmas season. In their home they have Christmas decorations. Every year in the sanctuary of their church, the story of the birth of Christ is reenacted to an overflow congregation, complete with a real baby. One Christmas eve the baby in the manger cried so lustily that he was taken out of the sanctuary so we could hear the choir. One year Sydney was one of two angels who proclaimed the birth of Christ from the church balcony.

It was in first grade that Lucas's belief in Santa Claus was challenged. One of his friends had told him there is no Santa Claus. I began to respond to his question.

"Well, Lucas, Santa Claus is a real game that parents and children love to play together at Christmastime. The story may have started with a real man, but it has been told so often that we cannot separate historical fact from what was added to the story along the way." Lucas's broad smile and nod indicated that he approved of the answer, and the conversation turned to other subjects.

Several years later Lucas asked, "Grammy, is God a game that parents play with children, like Santa Claus?" Eight–year-old Sydney came in from her bedroom and joined in the conversation.

I think the questions children have are important, and deserve our most thoughtful responses. Even as a small child I had a lot of questions of a theological nature. We have an 8 mm movie of Dad and me planting a garden, I think in the early spring of 1942, when I was in grade one. I remember our conversation as we were planting peas. Information about World War II filled the newspapers; we sang patriotic songs in school; our teachers encouraged us to support the war effort. I asked my Dad if the garden we were planting was a Victory Garden. He said no. I was disappointed. I asked him how our garden was different from a Victory Garden, then. He said that words matter, and what you called your garden was important. Victory gardens were part of the war effort. We were citizens of the Kingdom of God, he said, and the Kingdom of God is different: the children of God are peacemakers, the salt of the earth, children of light. Even in wartime, that is where our efforts should go. And I knew he was right.

In my first grade class at school I had a friend whose family received word that her 18-year-old brother had died in the European theatre of war. They were comforted by the knowledge that he'd been killed in action, defending his country and his family. And I knew they were right.

I had many theological questions that arose from my experiences, and my Dad always tried to provide answers that were rational, in words that I could understand: sometimes in stories, sometimes with reasoning. His sermons were filled with stories from the Bible and sometimes illustrations from our family life.

Sometimes when I asked my mother questions, she would say: "Well, honey, I don't know. We will just have to wait until we get to heaven and ask Jesus." From her I learned that there are many questions that we cannot answer.

The stories I was told at home and in church were responses to questions that went beyond my experiences and understanding. I don't think it mattered to me whether the stories were factual; it mattered that I understood the point the story was making. The stories gave me insight into who I was, how I came to be. They gave me energy and meaning. They illustrated mysteries and puzzles, such as the origins of humans, or of the universe. The stories may have begun with an historical incident, but may have been embroidered with details over time, and modified in retelling to reflect the changing understandings of humans over generations.

There are certain fundamental questions that every generation seeks to answer. Many questions remain the same; the answers vary with

the human knowledge available to each generation.

Joseph Campbell says that to ask the question
"Is God real?" is to project anthropomorphic con-
cepts and words into a sphere in which they do
not belong. We do this because we are human,
we want answers, and we process the information in which we are immersed in the only ways
that humans can. We speak of the hand of God, or
God as a Father, or a Mother. We see the universe as having a superior design, and think that
must mean that there is a Designer. Are these
ideas impediments to understanding the reality
in which we live? Or are they the best ways humans have found so far to explain how they fit
into a larger Reality?

"Man cannot maintain himself in the universe without some arrangement of the general
inheritance of myth," writes Campbell. Stories
can take us beyond the reality we experience to
the beginning understanding of a transcendent

reality. We are not as great as our aspirations. Our reach exceeds our grasp.

THREE HAIKU

There's more than PD

There is music and laughter

There's you and there's me.

In this small book are

People I remember and

You can know them too.

Having been larger,

I am now diminished.

What have I become?

GOD ATOMS

"Emergent phenomena"—that's what Bob called it when he spoke to the small group of women and men who were our church that Sunday afternoon. He told us that although no single atom could ever be thought of as having a temperature or a pressure, when large collections of atoms bump into each other, properties like temperature and pressure emerge. He referred us to Nancy Ellen Abrams's *A God That Could be Real: Spirituality, Science and the Future of the Planet*.

Bob was looking for a definition of God that is consistent with present day understanding of the universe. Abrams provides such a definition. Abrams says that emergent phenomena are real. They function as a higher order and persist beyond the lifetime of their constituent parts. She says God arises from human aspirations, is real, and persists over time. God functions as a higher order because of the interaction of the smaller component pieces, humans. On their own, the atoms would exhibit none of the properties of the higher order. In emerging, something new and unpredictable appears. This explanation of God is given within a framework of hard science, a framework that has the potential to explain the emergence of a real, transcendent God in a human world.

A year ago, the little country church of which I was a member closed for lack of members. At the same time, a group of residents in the retirement community where I now live were considering coming together as a new fellowship. I wondered, what makes a church a church? I listened to Bob and thought that the Church could be an emergent phenomenon that we have yet to understand. Bob was looking for a definition of God that is consistent with our present-day understanding of the universe. Abrams provides such a definition. Abrams says that emergent phenomena are real: they function as a higher order and persist beyond the lifetime of their components.

My search has not been for a real God. It seems to me that any human or group of humans who set out to define or describe God provide propositions that define the conclusion: "This God is possible because he meets the criteria I've established." My life experiences lead me to believe that there is energy in the universe and also in my life that I do not understand and cannot explain. I think my search has been for the Church.

What have I been hearing all of my life from my religious tradition? Stories of God's presence in people's lives and the difference it makes to the people—"God's people." Examples from the Hebrew tradition include the exodus of the children of Israel from Egypt, David and Goliath, Daniel in the lion's den, and Shadrach, Meshach, and Abednego. From the Christian tradition, the two disciples walking on the road to Emmaus and the story of Pentecost, the gathering in Jerusalem when the church was born.

But of course that was from the mythic dimension of our religious experience. Those things didn't really happen, some will say. And I don't think that matters. For me, whether it happened is not as important as: what is this story telling me? What questions are asked? What answer is the storyteller providing in his own time? Do the questions and answers apply to my time? To my life? I think that, in my search for the church, I would like to find stories that really happened, but, more than that, I want to find stories that provide meaning in life and death; stories that are so relevant and powerful that they can provide understanding, motivation for action, courage, acceptance and peace. I have begun to look again at the stories that we tell in our homes and in the places we call church.

My son-in-law Todd was returning from a conference on the west coast when the jet he was in hit severe turbulence. It was tossed around violently; Todd said it was like a ride on a roller coaster. Fear silenced the as white-knuckled passengers clung tightly to their armrests.

Suddenly a peal of child's laughter sounded throughout the cabin. The plane dropped again and a young child broke out in a belly laugh. He was on a roller coaster. He laughed again, and shouted, and Todd said his laughter was infectious and the cabin was filled with the laughter of adults. That's a transcendent experience. Todd was still amazed by that experience when he described it to us the following weekend.

Whatever I do with the rational, I want to live with the lyrical. I want it to motivate and inspire me. I do not know if I will develop a clearer understanding of God. I don't want to build an organization; I want to experience a Church. Can the church of our aspirations become a reality? The idea of emergent phenomena gives me hope.

THE PEACEABLE CORNER

For years the corner of Poplar Grove Street and Edmondson Avenue in west Baltimore has been a center of drug activity and violence. The corner is a commercial area: takeout food is served from behind bullet proof windows, and liquor stores serve as gathering places for men with time on their hands. Sun-faded advertisements are taped to windows of various local small business ventures. White faces are few and far between.

When there was a call for a nonviolent presence on Baltimore streets in the summer of 2013, Hunting Ridge Presbyterian Church members went to that corner, determined to provide an alternative to the violence that would not go away. Our message? That God came into our world in human form to teach us a different way to live together.

Joan joined us on the Corner after she retired from a successful career in office management. One afternoon, on a day when we had brought some cookies and juice and there was enough for everyone on the corner, she said, "This is just like the five loaves and two fishes."

I knew what she was talking about. Being on the Corner is the closest I have been to being in the presence of the teacher of Galilee. At the Corner I look across the street and see the large Western Cemetery, and I think of the Valley of Kidron outside the wall of Jerusalem. The Corner is on the crest of a hill, and I think of the Mount of Olives where Jesus and his followers gathered to talk and pray. In west Baltimore, some distance from our corner, is an historic public bath that was built in 1901. I think of the pool of Siloam, outside the wall of Jerusalem, where families would bring those needing healing. I look at the city police presence and think of the Roman soldiers who maintained a military presence to keep the peace.

Stories of Jesus' ministry come to mind, and sometimes I imagine a Baltimore story from Luke:

Soon afterward he went on through west Baltimore down Edmondson Avenue to Catonsville and Ellicott City, proclaiming the good news of the kingdom of God. In the crowd following Jesus were disciples from Hunting Ridge and other churches and people from the corner...

We cannot destroy the evil in our land by beefing up our police force or withdrawing to a safer place. Only by being an alternative in a place where the people find too few alternatives can we make a way to peace and safety together. The people on the corner are the people of the land, the same who flocked around Jesus two thousand years ago. Their curiosity led them to notice a different gathering, and come together at an intersection, at the top of a hill. We need to be where they are.

WHEN REASON ENDS

When reason ends
There is rest in song,
Love in the touch of a hand,
Forgiveness in an embrace.

Reason cannot know
The unknowable
Beginning and ending.

Reason cannot claim
Reward for righteousness or
Pardon for good intentions.

When reason ends
There is the beauty of being and
We live in the flow of I am,
Together.

CHRISTMAS, 1941

Winters were frigid in Stayner, Ontario. In autumn the wind became cold, and by December the ground was frozen and there was snow in the air and on the ground. During the day my sister, Iva, and brothers, Harold and Arthur, were in school, and I played inside at home. Dressing to go outside became quite a chore. Coats had to be thick and warm. They were hard to button. Hats had to cover your ears. Scarves had to be wrapped around your neck so the snow didn't get inside. Boots came up to your knees and you had to put a piece of paper on the heel of your shoe to slip it into the heel of your boot. Mittens were pinned to your coat or connected by a knitted cord that ran through your coat sleeves.

Christmas was a special time in our church and in our home. We read Luke's Christmas story and sang carols. My mother, who'd grown up Methodist Episcopal, taught me some Christmas songs that she learned in the little English community of West Berlin, New Jersey. I especially liked "Jolly Old Saint Nicholas, Lend Your Ear This Way." Brother Arthur wrote new words for old carols, but I was the only one who sang "While shepherds washed their socks by night" with him.

The focus of the Christmas celebration in our family was the message that the angels had brought the shepherds, but on Christmas morning I couldn't wait to see what Santa had brought to me. After we opened our Christmas gifts and had a breakfast of hot chocolate and toast, Dad went out to start the '37 Ford. We bundled up in warm clothing and piled into the car. The seating arrangement was well established: each brother claimed a window; my sister sat in the middle; I sat in the front seat between our parents. As we travelled we played alphabet geography, and counted cows and horses and then buried them when we passed a graveyard. In two hours we were at Fairview Farm, where years ago my dad was born, the first of nine children. We always returned with Dad and Mom to celebrate Christmas on the farm.

In the 1700s Casper Schuerch travelled from Switzerland to Holland and set sail from Rotterdam for the colony of Pennsylvania. I am told that his story is chronicled in the legal archives of the colony of Massachusetts, and includes a devious captain who would not bring the ship to land because he wanted to claim his passengers' belongings after they died. There was a shortage of food and much illness onboard. Two thirds of the passengers died, including Casper's wife and infant son. After a mutiny, the ship was brought to the closest harbor, Martha's Vineyard in Massachusetts.

Casper settled in Lancaster County, Pennsylvania. After the Revolutionary War, his grandson, Josef, left Lancaster County to settle in Waterloo County, Ontario. Josef Schuerch's stone farmhouse, built beside the Grand River, is today a bed and breakfast enterprise. Josef's grave is nearby, at the base of the Pioneer Memorial Tower. Grandma Sherk was a descendant of another pioneer, Josef Schneider, who established a lumber mill on his farm, which is now Victoria Park in Kitchener, Ontario. Dad travelled as far as India in his lifetime, but Waterloo County, Ontario was always home to him.

Christmas was a time for the uncles to show off their cars. Dad bought an 8mm movie camera in 1941, and he wanted to film "The Gathering of the Clan" at Christmas. Our family arrived at the farm early, and we children had to watch for the appearance of the uncles' cars and call Dad so he could take pictures, starting with each family getting out of their car and carrying packages and food and little children into the house. Second-born Uncle Eldon and Aunt Aleda were first to appear. Five-year-old Gordon scampered up the walk; Willard was a baby in his mother's arms. Uncle Floyd and Aunt Marjorie brought the always-well-behaved Marian (who was two years younger than I), Vernon, Catherine, and the twins, Alan and Alice. Charming Aunt Olive and her English husband, Eric Bolton, greeted the delighted children. Aunt Grace (who was full of grace and love) and Uncle Victor had three sons: Elverne, Cecil, and Percy. Wayne, also known as Snookie. was not yet born. I don't know where Uncle Paul was—maybe he was courting Aunt Norma, with whom he was to have five children: Cathy, John, Betty, Bob, and Norma Jean. Aunt Isabel, the youngest of Dad's siblings, who would marry Uncle Herb on V-J Day, was organizing the meal in the kitchen. Isabel and Herb would have four children: Esther, Anne, John, and Miriam. This list of names is important; everyone wanted to know where you fit in. (My brother Arthur would pray for each one of his children and grandchildren by name.)

The farmhouse filled with the wonderful smells of Christmas: the fresh-cut Christmas tree, roast turkey and stuffing, ham, yams, mashed white potatoes with gravy, vegetable casseroles, and molded salads. Baked goods, Christmas cookies and homemade candy awaited. One large T-shaped table filled the living and dining room. There was a table for the oldest children. There was a place for all.

We sat in our chairs and bowed our heads. Grandpa led the family in a prayer of thanksgiving, and Grandma's face glowed with love. At each place setting there was a Christmas cracker that we opened with a snap, and inside was a tiny toy and a colorful hat made of tissue paper. The Christmas meal was traditional southern Ontario Pennsylvania Dutch cooking at its finest. It really schmecked! When the meal had been consumed and everyone was feeling full and drowsy it was time to sing. Grandpa and Grandma's progeny had a great love of harmony, rhythm, and family. The afternoon was filled with music and laughter. The children played together and the men talked and as they sang, the women quietly cared for their children and cleared the tables.

But it was starting to get dark. These days were the shortest of the year. Some uncles had to get home to milk the cows. In short time children and leftovers were packed into cars. I don't remember putting on my overcoat and hat. I don't remember the ride home. There were no cows or horses or cemeteries. There was the sound of the car engine and the crunch of tires on snow-covered roads and then there was sleep. When I awoke the sun was up, I was home in my bed, and it was Boxing Day.

AFTERWORD

These are some of the songs of my life. I have given dates and names and experiences as they were told to me and as I remembered them. Some of my songs are in a minor key, some in a major key, but they all have meaning and depth, and need to be shared.

The stories are written. Life goes on. But what I have written here is not in the past. I'm thinking of that conversation with my Dad in the garden that wasn't a Victory Garden. Words matter.

I need to stop writing now. But somebody needs to take it further.

Mildred Sherk Kreider was born in 1936 in the rural township of Sunnidale, Ontario. Her education began in public schools in Ontario, and continued in the United States. She graduated from Goshen College in northern Indiana in 1958 with a B.S. in Nursing. She earned an M.S. in Nursing from the University of Maryland, Baltimore and a PhD in Education from the College of Education, University of Maryland, College Park. She was on the faculty of the University of Maryland School of Nursing for 25 years. After retiring, she earned an M.A. in Theology from the Ecumenical Institute of St. Mary's Seminary, Baltimore, and was an elder of the Presbyterian Church for 20 years. She was married to Sidney Kreider for 33 years. They have two children: Tim, a writer, and Mary Elizabeth, a doctor of pulmonary medicine.

79043503R10078

Made in the USA
Columbia, SC
18 October 2017